Love to Sew

Crazy Garlands & Bunting

Dedication

I would like to dedicate this book to my
Mum and Iain.

Love to Sew

Crazy Garlands & Bunting

Alistair Macdonald

Search Press

First published in Great Britain 2014

Search Press Limited
Wellwood, North Farm Road,
Tunbridge Wells, Kent TN2 3DR

Text copyright © Alistair Macdonald 2014

Photographs by Paul Bricknell at Search Press studios

Photographs and design copyright © Search Press Ltd. 2014

ISBN: 978-1-84448-999-2

The Publishers and author can accept no responsibility for any consequences arising from the information, advice or instructions given in this publication.

Suppliers
If you have difficulty in obtaining any of the materials and equipment mentioned in this book, then please visit the Search Press website for details of suppliers:
www.searchpress.com

Acknowledgements

Alistair would like to thank the team at Search Press, including Katie French and Daniel Conway for editorial support, Paul Bricknell for the beautiful photography, Juan Hayward and Marrianne Miall for staging and styling, and everyone supporting me by buying a copy of my book – I hope you have enjoyed it!

Printed in China

Sausage String, page 20

Pink and Fluffy, page 22

Counting Sheep, page 28

Pixie Toadstools, page 30

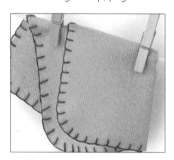

Spring Cleaning, page 36

Big Buttons, page 38

Festive Fun, page 48

Seaside, page 50

Contents

Ballerina, page 24

Rain or Shine, page 26

Retro Disco, page 32

Chinese New Year, page 34

Gingham Fruit, page 40

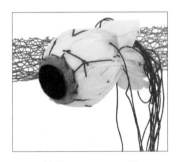

Halloween, page 42

Set Sail, page 44

Hot Air Baloons, page 46

Flower Pots, page 52

Winter Garland, page 54

Sporty Garland, page 56

Dream Land, page 58

Introduction

Bunting and garlands have to be among the most versatile decorations – whatever the occasion, the world over!

From the humble village fair to grand state visits, *Crazy Garlands & Bunting* brings a whole new meaning to the long-serving, triangular-shaped flag. There is no limit to the wild and wacky creations you could make, so why limit yourself? Join me on this fun-filled sewing adventure!

Garlands can be made from virtually anything and are a fantastic way of using up the old fabric scraps and hoarded bits and pieces that many of us just cannot bear to part with. A good stash of fabrics, trims, buttons and anything crafty can turn the plain into the delightfully crazy!

In this book there is something for everyone – young or old, boy or girl. Make light work of laundry day with the 'Spring Cleaning' bunting, have a guilt-free breakfast and sew it instead with a 'Sausage String' or simply curl up under the duvet and drift off to 'Dream Land'. With easy step-by-step instructions to guide you and twenty designs, you will be spoilt for choice. I hope you will be making and hanging garlands everywhere!

The projects are easy to follow and are accompanied by templates. You really don't have to be a professional – just have a go and be creative. Turn your piles of fabric and jars of buttons into something amazing.

Alistair Macdonald

Materials & equipment

To make the projects in this book, all you need is a stash of materials and some basic equipment. A good pair of hands and a sharp pair of scissors is the best place to start. A sewing machine can be bought for little money these days and you really don't need anything fancy. As long as it will perform the basics, you're in business.

Sewing machine

Most of the projects in this book require the use of a domestic sewing machine. Look for a good all-rounder with a small selection of stitches. A machine with a straight stitch, zigzag and buttonhole function is a good place start. Sewing machines can vary in price and function so only spend as much as you can afford.

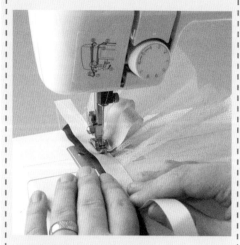

Fabrics

If you are anything like me, you will already have a stash of fabric all over the house – some new and some old, just waiting to be transformed. As you will see throughout this book, bunting can be made from virtually anything. Fabrics are, of course, all different: colour, texture, composition and weight. Fabric weight can be split into three main categories:

- Lightweight – chiffon, muslin, voile and lawn.
- Mediumweight – cotton shirting, satin, silk, flannel and linens.
- Heavyweight – canvas, denim, corduroy and wool.

Heavyweight fabrics such as denim and canvas are used to construct hardwearing things such as winter coats and upholstery. Mixing as many of these weights together as possible can lead to some exciting results. I always have a good stock of plain and patterned cottons, netting, wadding/batting, wool, felt and fleece, to name just a few, as you never know what you will need when the moment takes you. Fabric need not cost the earth either. Charity/thrift shops and markets may well be full of bargains.

Threads

Thread is another absolute must for any stitcher. Threads come in all different colours and sizes. It is always a good idea to have a selection of coloured sewing threads for hand and machine sewing. Embroidery thread is ideal when appliquéing and embroidering decorative stitches. Stranded embroidery cotton can be divided to form smaller strands for finer work.

Embellishments

Throughout the projects I have used a wide variety of embellishments, ranging from buttons and sequins to fake pearls and pompoms, all of which can be bought in any local craft store, sewing supplier or market.

Sewing needles

Sewing needles, both hand and machine, are vital for any sewing project. Most supermarkets and convenience stores will stock a pack of household needles. These packs usually contain a good variety of needles, ranging from sharps to embroidery, and they are normally at an affordable price. For machine needles, visit your local craft store, sewing supplier or buy online.

I have discovered doll-making needles, which are amazing. These are super-long and can thread thicker threads, too. This is ideal when you need to sew through a round shape or very thick layers.

Pins

They come in all shapes and sizes and are a stitcher's best friend! Be careful when using ones with coloured tips as these can be plastic and should not be used with an iron.

Iron

Every household should have one. A good steam function is useful.

Fabric punch

To punch out holes in fabric. When punching, add a piece of extra fabric or card to the underside for a clean cut.

Opposite:
Clockwise from top left
Top row: assorted yarns and ribbons; cotton rope and piping cord.
Second row: fake pearl trim; cotton ribbons and woven trim; pompoms; chenille pipe cleaners and popsicle sticks.
Third row: coloured embroidery threads; cream grosgrain ribbon; orange lace/netting ribbon; floral bias binding and large polystyrene/styrofoam balls.
Fourth row: buttons; gold studs; ric rac braid; small polystyrene/styrofoam balls and marabou feathers.
Bottom row: small, fake pearl-beads; loose, dried lavender and wobbly eyes.

Knitting or upholstery needles

Very useful for teasing out fabric corners when you have turned your work through. Please use the blunt end of the upholstery needle and store with the sharp end inserted into a cork.

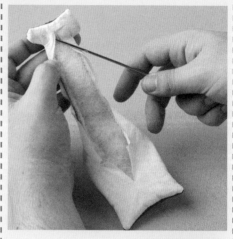

Glue gun

For instant and secure bonding. Always place the gun on a surface protector (cardboard will do) and never leave unattended. The glue will be hot, so mind those fingers and remember to keep a few refill glue sticks handy.

Pompom maker

Pompom makers can be purchased in craft stores in various sizes.

Other materials and equipment

You will need a range of cutting equipment. Sharp fabric scissors, thread snips, paper scissors, wire snips, craft knife (this is optional), rotary cutter and cutting mat (again, optional).

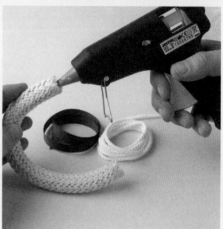

Toy stuffing is ideal for stuffing projects. An allergy-free option for stuffing is kapok – a 100% natural plant fibre. This can be quite hard to find these days and is much more expensive than polyester versions.

A good 150cm (59¼in) long tape measure in a vivid colour (easier to find in a creative mess!) and a 30cm (12in) clear ruler are all you need to sew your way through this book.

For marking cloth, my number one choice is a sharp piece of tailor's chalk. When you want to remove the chalk, rub it with a scrap of the same cloth and always keep a chalk sharpener handy (see yellow sharpener pictured opposite). Brushes can be too harsh and unsettle the surface of the fabric. Pencils and disappearing pens are another good choice, but always test them on a spare piece of your project fabric before use.

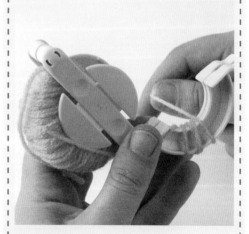

Transferring templates onto craft paper/card can be done in many ways. I like to use a tracing wheel. A tracing wheel has lots of little spikes, which leave holes wherever it has been applied. Simply enlarge the template you wish to copy and copy it onto some card/paper and draw around it with the wheel. Once you lift the original off, you will see a perforated copy transferred onto the card (make sure you trace onto a cutting mat to protect your surface). A top tip is to save cereal boxes, as the card from these make great templates.

For some of the projects in this book you will also need bulldog clips, craft wire, and a handy thimble.

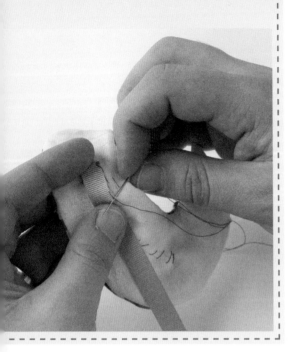

Basic techniques

Some of the basic techniques you will need are outlined here with simple step-by-step instructions.

Most of the sewing techniques used in these projects are easy to follow and require only a basic level of skill. Be sure you have fabric scissors, pins and your sewing machine handy! All the templates for the designs can be found on pages 60–64.

Appliqué

1 Position your felt appliqué on the front of your fabric, pin in place. Thread your needle through from the back of the fabric and begin to stitch.

2 Continue stitching around the appliqué, keeping an even distance from the edge. Pull through to finish at the back of the piece and secure with a few stitches.

Starting and finishing a thread

1 Pass the thread through a little way from your starting point.

2 Come out at your starting point and pull tight until the tail end of the thread vanishes underneath the fabric.

3 Stitch as the project requires, in this case along the edge.

4 Cast off by making a loop and passing the thread through to form a knot.

5 Pull the knot tight and pass the needle back through the fabric.

6 Cut some distance away from the end of the thread to finish.

Stitching around a shape and turning through

1 Stitch around the edges of two layers of fabric, right sides facing.

2 Clip round the curves, snipping 'v' shapes to just short of the stitching line and trim excess fabric all round the edges. This will make a neater finish once you turn through.

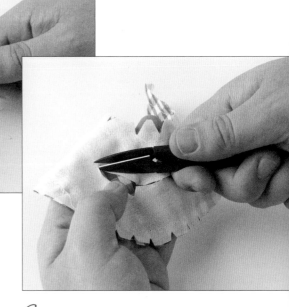

3 Cut a slit in the back and turn through so the piece is right sides out.

4 Push out the corners using a knitting or upholstery needle.

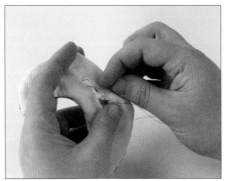

5 Loosely stitch the two sides of the slit closed, using a large stitch and being careful not to stitch through the front of the fabric.

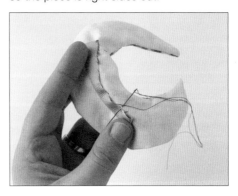

6 Position a length of grosgrain ribbon over the slit and stitch in place to finish.

Making a pompom

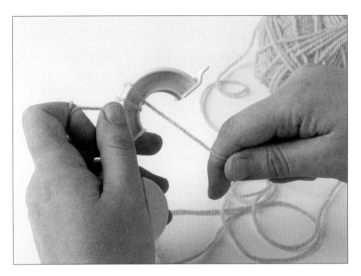

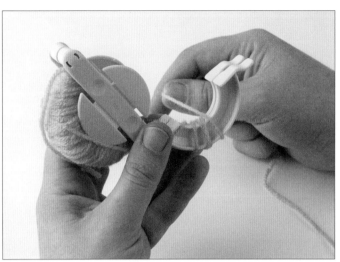

1 Wrap the yarn around one half of the pompom maker.

2 Continue wrapping until you have a created a thick layer, then start wrapping yarn around the other half.

3 When finished, close up the pompom maker and cut through all the yarns.

4 Wrap a length of yarn two or three times round the middle of the pompom maker. Pull tight and knot securely.

5 Release the pompom from the pompom maker and trim where necessary.

Projects

Garlands and bunting have never been so much in vogue and are a good way for sewing enthusiasts to hone their skills. The following pages are literally bursting with crazy garland projects for you to make, hang and enjoy. There is something for the whole family. Get those sewing machines ready, the scissors sharpened and tie your hair back – it's time to make garlands and bunting, the likes of which have never been seen before.

Please sew responsibly!

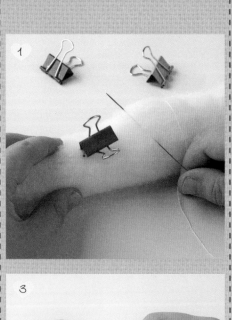

Sausage String

Materials

- templates for project on page 63
- 1 pair of tights/pantyhose – dark tan colour
- felt – red, yellow, white, pale pink, grey, dirty beige and burgundy
- wadding/batting 1cm (³⁄₈in) thick, 150 x 20cm (60 x 8in)
- 4 x cream/white netting, 9 x 9cm (3½ x 3½in) per tea bag
- loose lavender
- assorted small cream buttons
- embroidery threads – red, yellow, brown and white
- cotton yarn
- small yellow seed beads

Tools

- scissors (paper and fabric)
- sewing machine
- ruler
- hand sewing needles
- upholstery needle
- card or craft paper
- pins
- bulldog clips

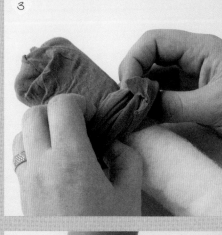

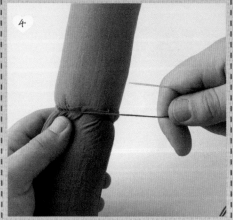

1 To make the sausages, lay the wadding/batting flat with the longest edge facing you and roll it evenly, tight enough to form a tube to secure the roll. Use small bulldog clips to temporarily hold it in place.

2 Using the upholstery needle and a large running stitch, sew the wadding/batting together. Remove the clips.

3 Cut off the top of the tights/pantyhose so that only the legs are left. Gather each end of the tights/pantyhose at the toe. Place one end of the wadding/batting roll into one of the toes and unroll this leg, encasing the wadding/batting. Secure the end with a running stitch to hold into position. Repeat the process with the other leg and from the opposite end of the wadding/batting roll. Ensure all of the wadding/batting has been hidden.

4 Use brown embroidery thread to secure the ends of the sausages by wrapping the thread around the roll at intervals of 15cm (6in), starting at the end where you secured the leg. Draw the thread in tightly and secure it in place, with a finishing stitch.

5 Copy the enlarged templates from page 63 onto card or craft paper and use them to mark and cut out the shapes in the appropriate colour felt. Cut two base sections each of the bacon, mushroom, fried egg and tomato. Layer the sections together and secure using a running stitch around the edge in matching thread. Appliqué the other shapes (bacon meat, tomato segments, mushroom top and stem and egg yolk) onto the base sections. To finish, add a decorative blanket stitch around the outside edges (stitch only at the top of the bacon to form the rind). Add seed beads to the tomato and buttons to the mushroom.

6 For each tea bag, mark and cut out four 9cm (3½in) squares of netting and pin together. Machine stitch around three of the edges, 1cm (⅜in) away from the edge. Fill with three teaspoons of lavender and machine sew the opening closed. To one corner, attach 15cm (6in) of doubled cotton yarn, tying a knot to secure at the other end. Cut out a white felt tab and fold in half. Sandwich the yarn between the felt and machine stitch closed. Make as many as you wish.

7 Attach all the components to your sausages using small tacking stitches around the edges of the pieces.

Pink and Fluffy

Materials

- ♥ templates for project on page 64
- ♥ pink marabou trim – measure to the required length of your garland, plus ties at the ends
- ♥ pink and purple sequin fabric or similar

Tools

- ♥ scissors (paper and fabric)
- ♥ sewing machine
- ♥ hand sewing needles
- ♥ upholstery needle
- ♥ card or craft paper
- ♥ pins
- ♥ fabric marker

1 Start by transferring the enlarged flag template (see page 64) onto some card or craft paper and cut out.

2 Fold the sequin fabric in half, right sides facing, and lay it on a flat work surface. Place the enlarged template on the cloth and draw round the edges with a fabric marker. Secure the two layers of the flag with pins and cut around the marked lines. Repeat this process until you have enough flags for your bunting length.

3 Set a sewing machine to a medium-sized stitch and sew down one of the sides. As you reach the end of the first side stop the stitching 1cm (⅜in) away from the base of the work. Lift the foot and turn the flag towards you. This will align the opposite side to continue stitching. Now trim the excess fabric from the tip of the flag and turn right side out using the blunt end of an upholstery needle to push the tip out to a sharp point. Press the flag flat and trim away the protruding seam allowance to maintain a straight edge along the top of the flag. Take extra care when pressing and use a cloth to protect any plastic sequins. Machine stitch the opening to close (this edge will be hidden by the marabou trim). Repeat this process for all of your flags.

4 Position the flags, evenly spaced along the marabou trim, with the raw edges touching the marabou. Pin to secure and make a small stitch at either end of each flag to secure it. As the marabou has a fluffy mind of its own, I find blowing onto it while stitching helps to reduce entanglement with the thread.

Ballerina

Materials

- ♥ template for project on page 60
- ♥ string of fake pearls – measure to the required length of your garland, plus ties at the ends
- ♥ 2 x pink netting, 12 x 40cm (4¾ x 15¾ in) per tutu
- ♥ pink and white felt
- ♥ burgundy satin ribbon, 4cm (1½ in) wide
- ♥ gold grosgrain ribbon, 1.5cm (⅝ in) wide
- ♥ cream grosgrain ribbon, 1cm (⅜ in) wide

Tools

- ♥ scissors (paper and fabric)
- ♥ sewing machine
- ♥ hand sewing needles
- ♥ upholstery needle
- ♥ card or craft paper
- ♥ pins
- ♥ pencil

1 Using the enlarged template from page 60, mark out and cut as many pairs of ballet shoes as you require from the pink and white felt. Place the white felt piece of the shoe on the pink shoe and pin to secure. Appliqué into position using a running stitch 5mm (¼in) from the white edge. Mark the position of the holes for the ribbon laces with a pencil. Thread the cream grosgrain ribbon onto an upholstery needle and lace up each shoe, starting from the toe and working towards the heel. Make sure you leave plenty of slack ribbon to tie and drape onto the pearls. Repeat for all shoes.

2 To make the tutus, pleat two layers of pink netting measuring 12 x 40cm (7¾ x 15¾in) per tutu along one of the long edges until you have reduced the netting to 15cm (6in) long. Cut a length of burgundy ribbon 17cm (6¾in) long and pin the net to the centre.

3 Machine stitch together along the edge of the ribbon. Turn in the cut ends of the ribbon to face the centre of the work and stitch in place. Fold the remaining ribbon edge over the net and machine stitch in place.

4 Cut a short length of the gold grosgrain and make two decorative loops. Add these to the base of the burgundy ribbon and stitch in place. Now add a single long piece of gold grosgrain to finish the waistband machine stitching in place at the top and bottom. Turn the loose ends towards the back and hand stitch down.

5 Attach the tutus to the pearls by tacking the waistband corners with burgundy thread. The shoes can be tied onto the pearls between the tutus by their ribbons. Drape the excess ribbon as if the ballerina had been in a whimsical hurry!

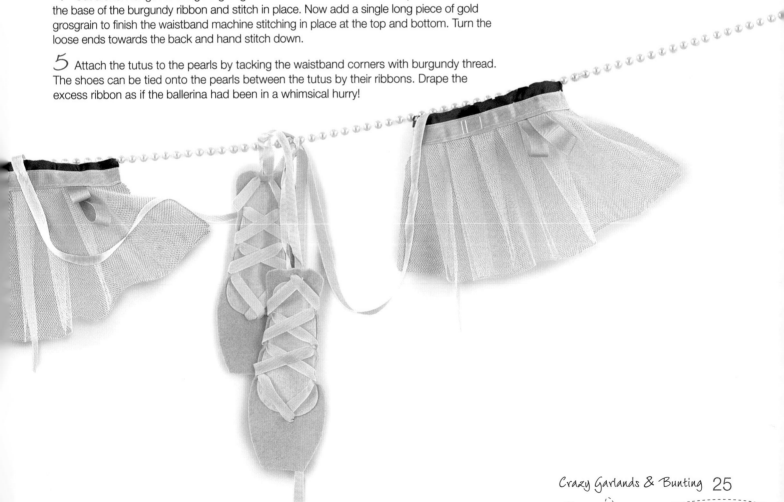

Rain or Shine

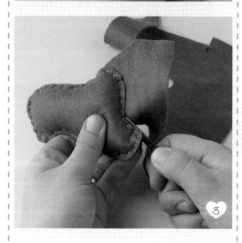

Materials

- ♥ templates for project on page 64
- ♥ ric rac braid, 4cm (1½in) wide –
  measure to the required length of your garland, plus ties at the ends
- ♥ felt – white, grey, red, blue, yellow and green
- ♥ matching sewing threads
- ♥ assortment of small white pompoms
- ♥ toy stuffing

Tools

- ♥ chalk
- ♥ scissors (paper and fabric)
- ♥ hand sewing needles
- ♥ card or craft paper
- ♥ pins

1 To make the clouds, use the enlarged templates and chalk to mark out as many small and large cloud shapes as needed on the white and grey felt (only mark out one side per cloud). Cut out, cutting inside the chalk lines. Pin these pieces onto another piece of felt in the same colour. Using a running stitch and matching thread, sew all round the perimeter of the cloud 5mm (¼in) away from the raw edge, leaving a 5cm (2in) gap for toy stuffing. NB: To make a lightning cloud, first cut out a lightning streak shape from yellow felt and pin the end to the inside of your cloud shape before sewing the two layers of cloud together.

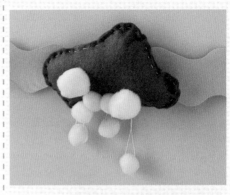

2 Lightly stuff the clouds until you are happy with the shape. To close, continue with the running stitch and secure when you reach the start of your stitching.

3 Once secured, use the pre-cut cloud as a template and cut the piece out. Repeat this for the rest of the clouds.

4 To make the sun, cut two circles of yellow felt using the enlarged sun template on page 64. Then cut five rectangle shapes of yellow felt to make your sunbeams. Position the rectangle shapes onto one of the circles and pin in place. Pin towards the centre of the circle to allow removal once stitched. Lay the remaining circle on top and work a line of running stitch 5mm (¼in) from the raw edge. Add a little stuffing before you close. To create the cloud layers, start with a large cloud and then add the sun and a little cloud, stitching them in place.

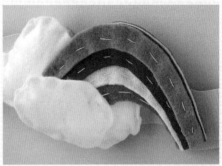

5 To make the rainbow, use the enlarged rainbow template from page 64 and apply the same layering. Secure the coloured layers using a large running stitch, following the shape of the rainbow. To create the cloud layers, start with a large cloud and then add the rainbow and a little cloud, stitching them in place.

6 To make the rain, cut out some raindrop shapes from blue felt and sew them onto the layered clouds with white sewing thread – allow some to dangle on threads to add extra character.

7 To make the snow cloud, sew on the small white pompoms with white sewing thread – allow some to dangle on threads to add extra character.

8 Pin the finished clouds to the ric rac braid and secure with tacking stitches. Now hang to brighten a room, come rain or shine.

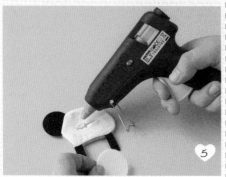

Counting Sheep

Materials

- ♥ template for project on page 60
- ♥ yellow bias binding 2.5cm (1in) wide – measure to your required length of your garland, plus ties at the ends
- ♥ A4 sheet (9 x 12in) of black felt (makes 9 sheep and two rows of Zs)
- ♥ scraps of white and light and dark green felt for sheep backs and grass
- ♥ long and short popsicle sticks
- ♥ cream cotton fabric for lining
- ♥ grey and beige fleece fabric, 10 x 7cm (4 x 2¾in) per sheep
- ♥ toy stuffing
- ♥ sewing threads to match the fleece fabrics
- ♥ yellow embroidery thread

Tools

- ♥ scissors (paper and fabric)
- ♥ glue gun
- ♥ sewing machine
- ♥ hand sewing needles
- ♥ upholstery needle
- ♥ card or craft paper
- ♥ pencil
- ♥ pins

1 Enlarge the template for the body of your sheep on page 60 and mark out as many sheep as you require on the cream cotton fabric and cut them out. Lay these, pencil side up, on the furry side of the grey and beige fleece fabrics and pin to hold.

2 For each sheep, cut out two legs and one head in black felt. Sandwich these pieces between the fleece and cotton, pointing towards the centre. Tack or pin to secure before sewing.

3 Machine stitch all around each sheep, leaving no opening. Cut round the stitch lines leaving a 5mm (¼in) seam allowance. Lightly clip the curves to avoid twisting when turning through.

4 With the lining side facing you, slash a straight line about 5cm (2in) long into the cotton with the fabric scissors. Turn the work through and use the blunt end of an upholstery needle to ease the sheep into shape.

5 To cover up the slashed opening, draw the fabric together with a large, rough stitch. Use a glue gun to stick a circle of white felt over the top to conceal the hole. For the fluffy hair, roll a small amount of toy stuffing between your hands to form a loose ball and glue it onto the head. Repeat this for all of the sheep.

6 Using the enlarged fence template on page 60, position the popsicle sticks to form the shape of the fence and stick them together with a glue gun. You may need to cut some of the sticks down. Cut the tufts of grass from scraps of green felt and glue onto the bottom of the fence posts. Position one of the finished sheep behind or in front of the fence as if it were jumping. Once you are happy with the placement, stitch or glue the sheep in place.

7 To make one row of Zs, cut out one 'Z' shape measuring 6 x 4.5cm (2½ x 1¾in), two measuring 4 x 3cm (1½ x 1¼in), and one measuring 2.5 x 2.5cm (1 x 1in) from black felt.

8 Carefully press the yellow bias binding in half, matching edge to edge. Set a sewing machine to a medium straight stitch and sew the bias closed as close to the edge as you can. Lay the binding flat and position the fences, the fence-jumping sheep and the Zs along it. Stitch in place. Position your flock of sheep and attach each one to the binding using yellow embroidery thread. Adjust the fall of each piece to mimic the herd jumping.

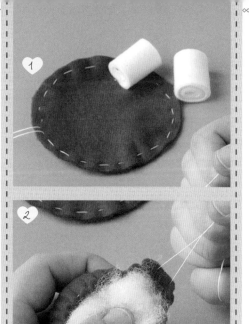

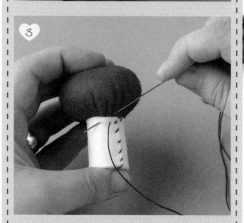

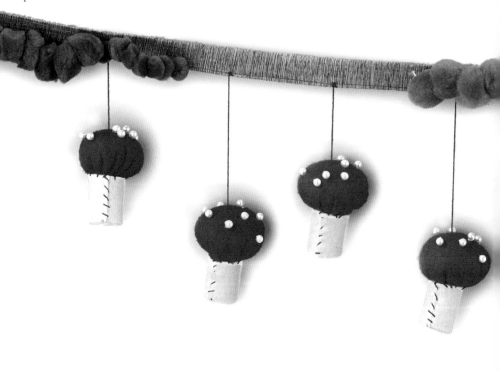

Pixie Toadstools

Materials

- ♥ template for project on page 61
- ♥ red felt, 12 x 12cm (4¾ x 4¾in) per toadstool top
- ♥ white felt, 3 x 34cm (1¼ x 13½in) per toadstool
- ♥ fancy brown and gilt ribbon 4cm (1½in) wide – measure to the required length of your garland, plus ties at the ends
- ♥ green pompoms, small to medium sizes
- ♥ small pearl beads approximately 4mm (⅛in), 7 per toadstool
- ♥ toy stuffing
- ♥ red embroidery thread
- ♥ matching sewing threads

Tools

- ♥ scissors (paper and fabric)
- ♥ sewing machine
- ♥ hand sewing needles
- ♥ card or craft paper
- ♥ tailor's chalk
- ♥ pins

1 Use the enlarged template on page 61 and some chalk to mark out on red felt as many toadstool tops as you require. Cut out inside the chalk lines. For each toadstool top, stitch a running stitch 5mm (¼in) from the raw edge of the piece. Leave the start and end of the threads loose, as these are used to gather the toadstool tops.

2 Draw the threads up to form a pouch. Fill this pouch tightly with toy stuffing and draw in further until the raw edges are almost touching. Tie to secure and flatten to form a domed toadstool top.

3 For the stalk, take a white felt piece and roll it up. Pin to hold. Using red embroidery thread, slip stitch along the raw edge of the felt and stitch onto the base of the toadstool top, covering the drawn hole.

4 Decorate the tops by sewing on pearl beads with white thread. Repeat steps 1 to 4 until all toadstools have been completed.

5 Carefully press the fancy ribbon in half lengthways, matching edge to edge. Set a sewing machine to a medium straight stitch and sew the ribbon closed as close to the edge as you can. Press flat. Lay the ribbon flat and position the toadstools along it. Attach each toadstool to the ribbon with red embroidery thread, varying the heights to form a random wave.

6 To form the caterpillars, simply thread the pompoms together. Start with the small ones and then add the medium. Once you are happy with the shape and the length, attach each caterpillar to the ribbon with a stitch in each end pompom and one somewhere in the middle.

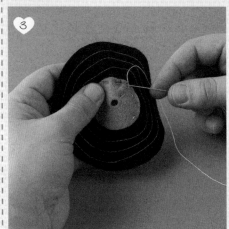

Retro Disco

Materials

- ♥ templates for project on page 61
- ♥ black felt, 12 x 12cm (4¾ x 4¾in) per disc and 10 x 6cm (4 x 2¼in) per music note
- ♥ assorted coloured felt scraps, 5 x 5cm (2 x 2in) per disc
- ♥ pink striped ribbon, 1.5cm (⅝in) wide – measure to the required length of your garland, plus ties at the ends
- ♥ white sewing thread

Tools

- ♥ scissors (paper and fabric)
- ♥ sewing machine
- ♥ hand sewing needles
- ♥ card or craft paper
- ♥ fabric punch
- ♥ tailor's chalk
- ♥ pins

1 Transfer the enlarged templates on page 61 onto card or craft paper and cut out. Place the enlarged templates on black felt and draw round them with tailor's chalk. Cut out, making sure you cut inside the chalked lines for neatness. Put to one side.

2 Thread your sewing machine with white thread. Take a disc and sew around the perimeter 5mm (¼in) away from the raw edge. The easiest way is to use the machine foot as a guide. Once you have sewn around the disc, lift the foot and cut away any loose threads. Now start a new stitch line, inside the first, using the previous stitching as the outside edge. Repeat this step until you have three stitched circles, each one smaller than the previous. Do not worry if the circles are not perfect as this adds to the 'groovy' feel of the discs.

3 Cut out the centres of the discs in as many different colours of felt as you can. Punch a hole in the centre of each circle and pin to the middle of each disc. Appliqué the centre to the disc using a running stitch 5mm (¼in) away from the raw edge.

4 Work a line of blanket stitch around each note in white thread.

5 Lay the pink ribbon flat and place the pieces in the desired positions. Pin to hold. Once you are happy with the placement, slip stitch the pieces onto the ribbon at the rear.

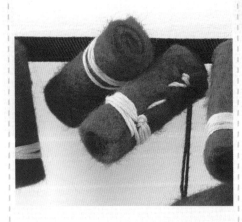

Chinese New Year

Materials

- ♥ red cotton fabric, 28 x 12cm (11 x 4¾in) per lantern
- ♥ red felt, 5 x 14cm (2 x 5½in) per lantern and 4 x 10cm (1½ x 5½in) per firecracker
- ♥ red grosgrain ribbon, 1cm (⅜in) wide – measure to the required length of your garland, plus ties at the ends
- ♥ red sewing thread
- ♥ red and gold/yellow embroidery threads

Tools

- ♥ scissors (fabric)
- ♥ sewing machine
- ♥ hand sewing needles

1 Using an iron, pleat the red cotton strips for the lanterns randomly until they measure 14 x 12cm (5½ x 4¾in). To hold the pleats in place, machine stitch along both longer edges, 5mm (¼in) from the edge. With the pleats facing vertically towards you, turn the side edges to the wrong side of the fabric by 1cm (⅜in) and stitch down (this hides the raw edges at the rear). Press flat.

2 Pin a strip of red felt along the raw edges of the right side, top and bottom. Machine stitch 1cm (³⁄₈in) away from this edge.

3 Fold the felt strip to the back of the pleated cotton along the stitching line and slip stitch down. When you reach the side edges of the felt, trim away the excess and stitch closed. The piece will now look like a flat square. To form the lantern shape, you will need to pinch each side of the cotton to make a horizontal fold where it joins onto the felt. Pinch around 10mm (½in), on the folded fabric, and sew down onto the felt at the back. Repeat until all four corners are pinched. You are aiming to give the felt a slight semi-circular curve.

4 To make the tassels wind red embroidery thread round three of your fingers. Tie the threads together with gold/yellow embroidery thread about 1cm (³⁄₈in) from one end, then snip open at the opposite end. Attach one tassel to the bottom of your lantern with a loop of red embroidery thread.

5 For the firecrackers, simply roll up a strip of pre-cut red felt like a cigar. With yellow/gold embroidery thread, slip stitch along the raw edge and then wrap the thread around the shape to form a band. Secure to finish. Repeat this step until you have a good pile. You can always make more if you run out.

6 Now you need to bring all of the elements together. Start by attaching the lanterns to the grosgrain ribbon using red thread. Suspend the lanterns away from the ribbon slightly and secure with a good knot. Lastly, attach the firecrackers along the entire length of the ribbon.

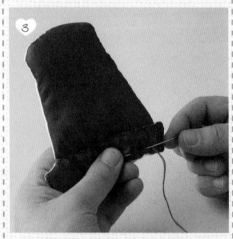

Spring Cleaning

Materials

- templates for project on page 61
- white piping cord/rope, approximately 1cm (³⁄₈in) thick –
  measure to the required length of your garland, plus ties at the ends
- A4 sheets (9 x 12in) of yellow, grey and green felt
- floral cotton, 23 x 14cm (9 x 5½in) per side of underpants
- 24cm (9½in) of 1cm (½in) wide yellow grosgrain ribbon per underpants
- 7 pink marabou feathers per feather duster
- toy stuffing
- burgundy felt strip 4 x 30cm (1½ x 11¾in)
- burgundy polyester silk, 15 x 17cm (6 x 6¾in)
- 1cm (³⁄₈in) thick wadding/batting, 15 x 17cm (6 x 6¾in) per bucket
- cream cotton fabric, 15 x 17cm (6 x 6¾in)
- scraps of white and blue felt
- 1 medium-sized green button
- wooden pegs
- red, orange, turquoise and green embroidery threads
- yellow sewing thread
- cream grosgrain ribbon, 1cm (³⁄₈in) wide
- cream cotton yarn

Tools

- scissors (paper and fabric)
- sewing machine
- hand sewing needles
- card or craft paper
- pencil
- pins
- upholstery needle
- glue gun

1 Using the enlarged templates on page 61 and a pencil, mark the bucket template on the cream cotton fabric, wadding/batting and burgundy polyester silk and cut out. Now create a sandwich as follows: wadding/batting, lining and cream cotton, pencil side up. Pin all layers together. Machine stitch all round, stitching 1cm (³⁄₈in) inside the pencil line. Do not leave an opening. Cut around the stitch lines leaving a 5mm (¼in) seam allowance. Lightly clip into the underarms of the bucket to avoid twisting when turning through.

2 With the cotton side facing you, slash a straight line about 7cm (2¾in) long with the fabric scissors. Turn the work through and use the blunt end of an upholstery needle to ease the bucket into shape. To cover up the slashed opening, draw the fabric together with a large rough stitch. Cover the drawn hole using the cream grosgrain ribbon. Slip stitch the ribbon in place for neatness.

3 Add some detail to the bucket by embroidering a running stitch around the top half about 5mm (¼in) away from the edge, using orange embroidery thread. Round off the strip of burgundy felt on one end.

4 Place the rounded end of the felt strip on the right-hand side of the bucket, then stitch on a green button, stitching through all layers. Secure the loose end at the back to form the handle. Cut out small circles from scraps of white and blue felt and stitch onto the bucket with white thread to simulate bubbles from soap suds. Place to one side.

5 To make the feather duster, trim down the sheet of grey felt to measure 25 x 21cm (9¾ x 8¼in) for the stick and a further piece 3 x 21cm (1¼ x 8¼in). Roll up the larger piece of felt to form the stick of the duster (the finished roll should be 25cm/9¾in long). To close, slip stitch along the raw edge with green embroidery thread. Using a glue gun, glue the 7 pink marabou feathers to one end of the stick. Once dry, attach the second strip of felt around the base, trapping and hiding the feathers inside. Cut back and slip stitch in place using black cotton thread. Add a cotton yarn loop to the end of the stick to finish.

6 To make the underpants, use the enlarged template to mark and cut out the back and front pieces on the floral cotton. Cut the yellow grosgrain ribbon to size, pin to the cotton in a 'Y' shape and machine stitch in place to the front of the piece. With right sides facing, pin the front and back pieces together and machine stitch 1cm (⅜in) away from the edge, leaving a 10cm (4in) gap for turning and stuffing. Clip and trim the seam allowance and turn through. Stuff the pants with toy stuffing and slip stitch the opening closed. Add a final strip of yellow grosgrain ribbon to the top to form a waistband, folding it over to the back for a neat finish.

7 Take the sheets of yellow and green felt, round off the corners of the yellow sheet and work large blanket stitch around the outside edge in red embroidery thread. Using the enlarged template mark and cut out the glove and blanket stitch all round in turquoise embroidery thread.

8 Position the pieces over the rope and secure with pegs. The bucket is the exception: this will need to be tacked into position along the handle's curve.

Big Buttons

Materials

- ♥ template for project on page 64
- ♥ assorted cotton gingham fabrics, 36 x 17cm (14¼ x 6¾ in) of folded fabric per flag
- ♥ brightly coloured large clown buttons, 6.5cm (2½in) in diameter
- ♥ blue bias binding 2.5cm(1in) wide – measure to the required length of your garland, plus ties at the ends
- ♥ white sewing thread
- ♥ embroidery threads in contrasting colours

Tools

- ♥ scissors (paper and fabric)
- ♥ sewing machine
- ♥ hand sewing needles
- ♥ card or craft paper
- ♥ tailor's chalk
- ♥ pins
- ♥ upholstery needle

1 Transfer the enlarged flag template from page 64 onto card or craft paper and cut out. Fold the gingham fabric in half, right sides together, and pin the layers together. Place the template on top and carefully draw round it. Remove the template and cut round the marked lines. Repeat this process until you have enough flags for your bunting length.

2 Thread your sewing machine with white thread. Take a flag and start to sew down one of the sides. As you reach the end of the first side, stop stitching 1cm (³⁄₈in) away from the base of the work. Lift the foot and turn the flag towards you. This will align the opposite side to continue stitching.

3 Trim the excess fabric from the tip of the flag (see page 16) and turn right side out. Use the blunt end of a large upholstery needle to ease the tip of the flag out (take care not to push too hard, as this may result in the needle coming through the work). Press the flag flat and trim away the protruding seam allowance to maintain a straight edge along the top of the flag. Repeat until all the flags have been completed.

4 Take the bias binding and carefully press it in half, matching the edges. Sandwich each flag between the folded binding and pin in position, spacing evenly and alternating the colours. Make sure you leave enough free binding at the start and end to allow for ties. Sew along the entire bunting length using a sewing machine set to a medium straight stitch. Stitch as close to the edge as you can. Press the bunting flat.

5 In the centre of each flag, hand sew a big clown button using embroidery thread. Both the thread and button should be a contrasting colour to the gingham flag.

Gingham Fruit

Materials

- templates for project on page 64
- assorted cotton gingham fabrics, 36 x 17cm (14¼ x 6¾ in) of folded fabric per flag
- scraps of yellow, orange and red felt
- blue bias binding, 2.5cm (1in) wide – measure to the required length of your garland, plus ties at the ends
- white sewing thread
- embroidery threads in contrasting colours
- embroidery threads

Tools

- scissors (paper and fabric)
- sewing machine
- hand sewing needles
- card or craft paper
- tailor's chalk
- pins
- upholstery needle
- glue gun (optional)

1 Transfer the enlarged flag templates from page 64 onto card or craft paper and cut out. Fold the gingham fabrics in half, right sides together and pin together. Place the template on top and carefully draw around all the edges using tailor's chalk. Remove the template and cut around the marked lines. Repeat this process until you have enough flags for your bunting length.

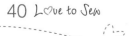

2 Thread your sewing machine with white thread. Take a flag and start to sew down one of the sides. As you reach the end of the first side, stop the stitching 1cm (³⁄₈in) away from the base of the work. Lift the foot and turn the flag towards you. This will align the opposite side to continue stitching.

3 Trim the excess fabric from the tip of the flag (see page 16) and turn right side out. Use the blunt end of a large upholstery needle to ease the tip of the flag out. Press the flag flat and trim away the protruding seam allowance to maintain a straight edge along the top of the flag. Repeat until all the flags have been completed.

4 Take the bias binding and carefully press it in half, matching the edges. Sandwich each flag between the folded binding and pin in position, spacing them evenly and alternating the colours. Make sure you leave enough free binding at the start and end to allow for ties. Sew along the entire bunting length using a sewing machine set to a medium straight stitch. Stitch as close to the edge as you can. Press the bunting flat.

5 To make the fruit motifs, transfer the enlarged templates on page 64 onto card or craft paper and cut out. Draw round the templates on the appropriate colour of felt and cut out. Add a blanket stitch along the perimeter of each fruit using a contrasting colour thread. Embroider small green leaves/stalks to the tops. Use a running stitch for the strawberry pips (curved lines) and French knots for the oranges and lemons.

6 Once you have completed the fruit, attach one to the centre of each flag by either slip stitching or gluing into position.

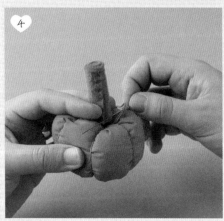

Halloween

Materials

- templates for project on page 61
- cream cotton fabric, 25 x 25cm (9¾ x 9¾ in) per ghost and 19 x 19cm (7½ x 7½ in) for the eyeball
- cream netting, 50 x 25cm (19¾ x 9¾in) netting per ghost
- orange cotton, 25 x 13cm (9¾ x 5in) per pumpkin
- 2 A4 sheets (9 x 12in) of black felt
- A4 sheet (9 x 12in) of green felt
- assorted black sequins
- wobbly eyes
- 4 black pipe cleaners per spider
- polystyrene/styrofoam ball per spider 4cm (1½in)
- polystyrene/styrofoam ball per eyeball 5cm (2in)
- orange lace/netting ribbon – 4cm (1½in) wide, measure to the required length of your garland, plus ties at the ends
- orange sewing thread
- toy stuffing
- green, black and red embroidery threads

Tools

- scissors (paper and fabric)
- sewing machine
- hand sewing needles
- glue gun
- card or craft paper
- tailor's chalk
- pins

1 Transfer the enlarged templates for the bat, ghost and eyeball on page 61 onto card or craft paper. Prepare as many elements as you wish for your bunting. Draw round your templates with tailor's chalk on their respective fabrics, cut them out and put to one side.

2 To make the pumpkins, bring the two shorter edges of the orange cotton together, pin and machine stitch closed. Secure a thread to one of the open ends 1cm (⅜in) from the edge and sew a running stitch all the way round. Pull the thread to gather. Wrap it tightly and secure. Turn the work inside out and fill with toy stuffing.

3 Sew a running stitch round the other opening in green embroidery thread, securing at the starting point. Draw tightly together and secure – but do not cut the thread. Take the needle through the entire shape from top to bottom. Now bring the thread up over the outside and back through the work. Pull taut. Work around the whole body in this way to form the sections of the pumpkin.

4 Cut a piece of green felt measuring 4 x 10cm (1½ x 4in) and roll up to form a stalk. Slip stitch closed and attach to the top of the pumpkin, hiding any raw edges. Finish by embroidering a jagged grin using black embroidery thread.

5 To make the spiders, cut a large black circle of felt, large enough to enclose one of the 4cm (1½in) polystyrene/styrofoam balls, and work a line of running stitch round it about 5mm (¼in) from the raw edge. Leave both the start and finish of the thread loose, as this will be used to help draw the felt closed over the ball. Place the ball in the centre and gather the felt around it. Once tight, tie to secure. Cut a smaller black circle of felt to cover the remaining exposed ball. Slip stitch into position. Use a glue gun to attach the pipe cleaners and wobbly eyes.

6 For the eyeballs, running stitch 2cm (¾in) away from the cream cotton circle's edge around the entire circumference, leaving both ends of the thread loose. Place a 5cm (2in) polystyrene ball in the middle and draw the cotton up around it. Pull tight and secure.

7 Glue the felt eye pieces onto the ball. With red embroidery thread, add some veins around the eyeball. Attach and leave some longer threads to make the eyeball look as if it has been ripped from its socket!

8 To make the ghost, start by layering the netting pieces over the cream cotton. Lay offset from each other and do not match the corners. Pin to hold. Mark the inner circle from the template. Apply a running stitch to this line and draw together. As you draw, add some stuffing into the circle to form the head. Draw in enough to hold the stuffing in place and tie to secure. Stitch on two large black sequins for the eyes and a smaller one for a mouth.

9 Now bring all of your elements together, not forgetting the bats, and sew them onto the orange lace/netting ribbon.

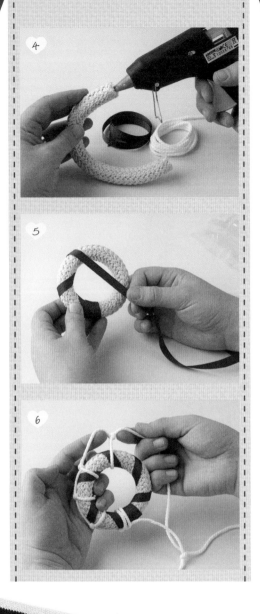

4

5

6

Set Sail

Materials

- ♥ templates for project on page 60
- ♥ red-and-white striped cotton, 34 x 15cm (13½ x 6in) of folded fabric per sail
- ♥ blue-and-white striped cotton, 34 x 15cm (13½ x 6in) of folded fabric per sail
- ♥ brown wool fabric, 16 x 10cm (6¼ x 4in) of folded fabric per boat
- ♥ 4 gold studs per boat
- ♥ popsicle stick per boat
- ♥ 24cm (9½ in) length of cotton rope, approximately 2cm (¾ in) in diameter per life ring
- ♥ red grosgrain ribbon, 1cm (⅜in) wide, approximately 70cm (27½in) length per ring
- ♥ piping cord, 3mm (⅛in), approximately 100cm (40in) length per life ring
- ♥ woven or knitted cotton trim with red, blue and white stripes – measure to the required length of your garland, plus ties at the ends
- ♥ white sewing thread
- ♥ cream grosgrain ribbon, 1cm (⅜in) wide

Tools

- ♥ scissors (paper and fabric)
- ♥ sewing machine
- ♥ hand sewing needles
- ♥ card or craft paper
- ♥ tailor's chalk
- ♥ pins
- ♥ adhesive tape
- ♥ glue gun

1 Transfer the enlarged boat and sail templates from page 60 onto card or craft paper and cut out. Fold the brown wool fabric in half, with right sides together, and mark out as many boats as you require using tailor's chalk. Remove the template and pin both layers together. Cut around the chalked lines. Repeat this step to mark and cut the sails from striped cotton.

2 To make the boats, pin the wool pieces right sides together and machine stitch around the outline of the pieces 1cm (⅜in) inside of the chalked line. Do not leave an opening. Cut around the stitch lines, leaving a 5mm (¼in) seam allowance. Clip away the corners and snip into the curves to avoid twisting when turning through. Slash a straight line about 7cm (2¾in) long in one side with fabric scissors. Turn the work through and use the blunt end of an upholstery needle to ease the boat into shape. To cover up the slashed opening, draw the fabric together with a large rough stitch. Cover the hole using the cream grosgrain ribbon. Slip stitch the ribbon in place for neatness. Turn the work over and add four gold studs along the straight edge (equal distance apart).

3 To make the sails, machine stitch the sails in a similar way, this time leaving an opening to turn through on one of the sides (ideally at the base of the sail). Turn through and press flat. Slip stitch the opening closed. Use a glue gun to attach a popsicle stick to the back of the sail and then glue the popsicle stick to the back of the boat at the centre.

4 To make the life rings, mark a 24cm (9½in) long piece of rope and apply some adhesive tape where you will cut; this will stop the rope fraying after cutting. Cut the rope, then glue the ends together.

5 Use this join as a starting point for the red grosgrain ribbon. Glue an end to this point and begin to wrap the ribbon around the whole ring. When you arrive back at the start, make sure you wrap more ribbon to hide any sticky tape and the join. Glue to secure at the rear.

6 Knot the piping cord onto the ring. Tie the cord round the ring, then take the loose end along the ring edge and tie round again. The effect should look like blanket stitch.

7 Pin the finished boats and life rings onto the woven cotton trim and stitch in place at the rear.

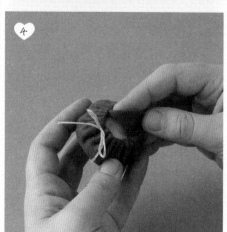

Hot Air Balloons

Materials

- ♥ templates for project on page 60
- ♥ assortment of plain, stripy and checked coloured cotton fabrics 22 x 12cm (8¾ x 4¾in) – four per balloon
- ♥ A4 sheet (9 x 12in) of brown felt (should make four baskets)
- ♥ toy stuffing
- ♥ bright yellow cotton webbing tape – measure to the required length of your garland, plus ties at the ends
- ♥ sewing thread
- ♥ yellow and orange embroidery threads

Tools

- ♥ scissors (paper and fabric)
- ♥ sewing machine
- ♥ hand sewing needles
- ♥ card or craft paper
- ♥ tailor's chalk
- ♥ pins

1 To make the balloons, transfer the enlarged template on page 60 onto card or craft paper and cut out. Place on the wrong side of the coloured fabric, draw around with tailor's chalk and cut out. Cut four pieces per balloon, in four different fabrics. Pin two of the cut-out shapes right sides together and machine stitch 1cm (³⁄₈in) from the edge. Always start stitching on the placement dot (this can be found on the pattern). Repeat with another two pieces. Now you have two halves. Simply bring these two halves together and stitch closed in the same way. You will now have a shape that resembles a tall hat. Clip the curves before turning through. Repeat until all balloons are at this point.

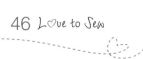

2 With the work turned through, fold the straight edge towards the centre until you are level with the fold line marked on the template. Pin to hold. With some tailor's chalk, mark the blue stitch line from the pattern as a guide. Work a line of running stitch along this guide line round the circumference, leaving both ends of the thread loose and on the right side of the balloon. Stuff with toy stuffing and gather tightly. Make sure this action does not trap any of the fabric below this line inside as this forms the bottom of the balloon. Tie off to secure.

3 Use the enlarged templates to cut out the basket circles. Take the large circle and apply a running stitch 5mm (¼in) away from the outside edge, using yellow embroidery thread. Leave these threads loose for drawing. Start to draw in the basket, add some stuffing to the middle and tie the threads to secure, leaving a good visible opening.

4 Cover the stuffing with the second smaller circle, hiding the edges within.

5 Suspend the baskets from the balloons at equal points using orange embroidery thread. Attach the finished balloons to the webbing tape in the same way. Alternate the balloon heights to give more interest.

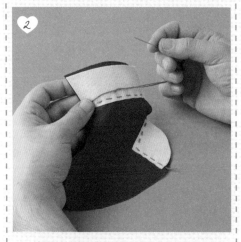

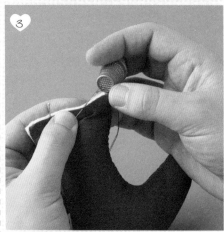

Festive Fun

Materials

- ♥ templates for project on page 63
- ♥ red cotton fabric, 34 x 15cm (13½ x 6in) per stocking
- ♥ scraps of ric rac assorted colours
- ♥ large green pompoms
- ♥ brown wool fabric, 17 x 14cm (6¾ x 5½in) per gingerbread man
- ♥ cream cotton fabric, 17 x 14cm (6¾ x 5½in) per gingerbread man
- ♥ wadding/batting, 12mm (½in) thick, 17 x 14cm (6¾ x 5½in) per gingerbread man
- ♥ yellow felt, 7 x 44cm (2¾ x 17¼ in) per crown
- ♥ white and red knitted braid, each 20cm (7¾in) long per candy cane
- ♥ red grosgrain ribbon, 1cm (³⁄₈in) wide, 10cm (4in) per candy cane
- ♥ white felt – half an A4 sheet (9 x 12in) makes two stockings
- ♥ christmas-coloured ribbon, 5cm (2in) wide – measure to the required length of your garland, plus ties at the ends
- ♥ toy stuffing
- ♥ craft wire
- ♥ pearls, 4mm (¼in) two per gingerbread man
- ♥ sewing thread
- ♥ white, red and green embroidery thread

Tools

- ♥ scissors (paper and fabric)
- ♥ sewing machine
- ♥ hand sewing needles
- ♥ wire snips
- ♥ card or craft paper
- ♥ tailor's chalk
- ♥ pins

1 To make a gingerbread man, use the enlarged template on page 63 and follow the instructions for steps 1 and 2 on page 36, using the brown wool fabric, cream cotton fabric and wadding/batting. Embroider running stitch in white all round the edge. For the decoration, add a scrap of ric rac round the neck and sew at the rear to secure. Embroider a couple of red stitches to form a mouth and two pearls for eyes.

2 To make the stockings, fold the red cotton in half, right sides together and draw round the enlarged template from page 63. Pin the two layers of fabric together to hold and cut out. Unpin and choose one of the pieces to be the front (this will determine the direction in which the stocking will face). Cut out the additional shapes in white felt from the stocking top and heel templates. Pin these in position and secure with a decorative running stitch in green embroidery thread.

3 Pin the stocking pieces right sides together and machine stitch around the piece, leaving the top of the stocking open. Trim away the excess seam allowance, turn through and fill with stuffing almost to the top. Fold 1cm (³⁄₈in) over along the top and slip stitch closed. Add a large green pompom to the toe of the stocking.

4 To make the candy canes, cut a length of craft wire with wire snips just a bit longer than the knitted braid. Make a loop at either end of the wire and insert into the red braid. Secure the loops at either end with a stitch. Twist one white braid along one red braid to form the stripes and stitch securely at the ends. Glue a little grosgrain ribbon around the ends for neatness and shape into a cane.

5 To make the crowns, use tailor's chalk to mark round the enlarged template from page 63 and cut out from yellow felt, cutting inside the lines. Make sure no chalk is showing. Bring the two ends together and stitch to secure either by machine or hand.

6 Lay the Christmas-coloured ribbon flat and arrange the gingerbread men, hats, stockings and canes in position. Once you are happy with the placement, pin and slip stitch securely at the rear of each piece.

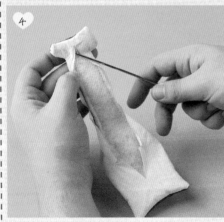

Seaside

Materials

- ♥ template for projects on page 62
- ♥ wadding/batting, 1cm (³⁄₈in) thick, 17 x 16cm (6¾ x 6¼in) per bucket, 24cm x 11cm (9½ x 4¼in) per spade and 22cm x 20xcm (8¾ x 7¾in) per starfish
- ♥ cream cotton fabric, 17 x 16cm (6¾ x 6¼in) per bucket, 24 x 11cm (9½ x 4¼in) per spade, 15 x 12cm (6 x 4¾in) per shell and 19 x 17cm (7½ x 6¾in) per sandcastle
- ♥ turquoise lining fabric, 17 x 16cm (6¾x 6¼in) per bucket
- ♥ hot pink lining fabric, 24 x 11cm (9½ x 4¼in) per spade
- ♥ orange cotton fabric, 44 x 20cm (17¼ x 7¾in) per starfish
- ♥ green felt, 4 x 30cm (1½ x 11¾in) per bucket
- ♥ beige fleece fabric, 19 x 17cm (7½ x 6¾in) per sandcastle
- ♥ grey fleece fabric, 15 x 12cm (6 x 4¾in) per shell
- ♥ popsicle stick
- ♥ one medium-sized button per bucket
- ♥ scraps of black and red felt
- ♥ black-and-white ribbon – measure to the required length of your garland, plus ties at the ends
- ♥ orange and grey embroidery thread
- ♥ cream grosgrain ribbon, 1cm (³⁄₈in) wide

Tools

- ♥ scissors (paper and fabric)
- ♥ sewing machine
- ♥ hand sewing needles
- ♥ glue gun
- ♥ pencil
- ♥ card or craft paper
- ♥ tailor's chalk
- ♥ pins
- ♥ upholstery needle

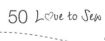

1 All of the elements that make up the seaside bunting are made in the same way. With a pencil, mark all of the enlarged templates from page 62 onto their respective fabrics. Now create a sandwich as follows: wadding/batting; main fabric (turquoise/hot pink lining fabric, orange cotton, beige or grey fleece, as appropriate); cream cotton, pencil side up. For the shell and sandcastle, leave out the wadding and place main fabric on the cream cotton, right sides together. Pin all the layers together.

2 Machine stitch around the whole piece 1cm (³/₈in) inside the pencil line. Do not leave an opening.

3 Cut round the stitch lines, leaving a 5mm (¼in) seam allowance. Lightly clip into the underarms of the bucket and the curves on the other pieces to avoid twisting when turning them through.

4 With the cotton side facing you, slash a straight line about 7cm (2¾in) long (this will be longer on the spade) with the fabric scissors. Turn the work through and use the blunt end of an upholstery needle to ease out the shape. To cover up the slashed opening, draw the fabric together with a large rough stitch. Cover the drawn hole using the cream grosgrain ribbon. Slip stitch the ribbon in place for neatness.

5 To embellish the bucket, embroider a running stitch around the top half about 5mm (¼in) away from the edge using orange embroidery thread. Take a strip of green felt measuring 4 x 30cm (1½ x 11¾in) and round off one end. Place the rounded end on the left-hand side of the bucket, then stitch on a contrasting button, stitching through all layers. Secure the loose end at the back; this will form the handle.

6 To embellish the starfish, use long stitches in orange embroidery thread to define the 'fingers' of the starfish. Start from the centre and work out to where each finger joins the next. Slightly pull these threads to achieve a more 3D effect. Tie off and pull in the tips of the fingers using orange embroidery thread. Embroider French knots for texture.

7 To embellish the shells, work long stitches in grey embroidery thread from the neck of the shell towards the outer edges. As with the starfish, use these stiches to shape the piece. At the edges add another stitch and pull taut, creating a scalloped edge.

8 To embellish the sandcastle, use the enlarged templates provided and cut out the door, flag and windows from scraps of black felt. Pin the door and windows in position and embroider a running stitch round the door and an X in the centre of each window using grey embroidery thread. Glue the flag to a popsicle stick and glue to the back.

9 Arrange the elements on your chosen ribbon and slip stitch to the rear to secure.

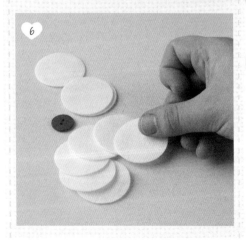

Flower Pots

Materials

- ♥ template for project on page 64
- ♥ brown wool fabric, 17 x 16cm (6¾ x 6¼in) per flower pot
- ♥ cream cotton fabric, 17 x 16cm (6¾ x 6¼in) per flower pot
- ♥ wadding/batting, 12mm (½in) thick, 17 x 16cm (6¾ x 6¼in) per flower pot
- ♥ green popsicle sticks
- ♥ bright-coloured medium-sized buttons
- ♥ 1cm (⅜in) thick cream grosgrain ribbon, 10cm (4in) per flower pot
- ♥ bright grosgrain ribbon, 40cm (16in) per flower pot
- ♥ A4 sheet (9 x 12in) of white felt, makes 20 petals (7 petals per pot)
- ♥ pale yellow bias binding, 2.5cm (1in) wide – measure to the required length of your garland (you will need two equal sized lengths of binding for this project), plus ties at the ends
- ♥ contrasting sewing thread

Tools

- ♥ scissors (paper and fabric)
- ♥ sewing machine
- ♥ hand sewing needles
- ♥ glue gun
- ♥ pencil
- ♥ card or craft paper
- ♥ tailor's chalk
- ♥ pins
- ♥ upholstery needle

1 To make the pots, take one piece of brown wool fabric per pot and draw on a grid of squares 2 x 2cm (¾ x ¾in) on the diagonal using tailor's chalk. This will give a diamond shaped finish on the pot. Place the wool, chalk side up, on the wadding/batting and work a large running stitch all round the outside edge of the two layers – this will stop them from sliding when you are quilting.

2 Set a sewing machine on a medium stitch length and topstitch over the marked lines using a contrasting thread for impact.

3 Using a pencil, draw around the enlarged plant pot template from page 64 on the cream cotton piece. Place each marked section pencil side up onto the quilted wool, matching all four corners, and pin to secure. Do not cut anything off at this stage.

4 Machine sew 1cm (⅜in) away from the inside of the pencil line. Cut around the stitch lines, leaving a 5mm (¼in) seam allowance. Lightly clip into the corners of the pots to avoid twisting when turning through. With the cotton side facing you, slash a straight line about 7cm (2¾in) long with fabric scissors. Turn the work through and use the blunt end of an upholstery needle to ease the shape out. To cover up the slashed opening, draw the fabric together with a large rough stitch. Cover the hole using the cream grosgrain ribbon. Slip stitch the ribbon in place for neatness.

5 Take a 40cm (16in) length of bright grosgrain ribbon. Fold it in half and sew 5cm (2in) from the middle to make a loop. Open out and attach the middle of the loop to this stitch line. Cover these stitches with a scrap of the same ribbon. You now have a bow to embellish your flower pot.

6 To make the flower heads, cut out six small white felt circles, 4cm (1½in) in diameter, and spread and overlap them into a round. Carefully glue a seventh circle into the centre to secure. Flip the work over and sew a bright button into the middle. Glue a green popsicle stick to the rear of the flower head and then glue the popsicle stick in position on the back of each pot. Lastly, machine sew the two lengths of pale yellow bias binding together as close to the edges as possible. Press flat. Position the flower heads along the binding and sew or glue them in place.

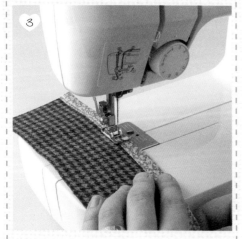

Winter Garland

Materials

- ♥ templates for project on page 64
- ♥ beige knitted ribbed jersey fabric 34 x 15cm (13½ x 6in) per hat
- ♥ thick blue checked wool fabric 59 x 8cm (23¼ x 3¼in) per scarf
- ♥ pink and blue knitted braid, 1m (40in) per pair of mittens
- ♥ white wool, 100g (3½oz)
- ♥ fancy bias binding 2.5cm wide, 110cm (43¼in) per scarf and 30cm (11¾in) per hat
- ♥ cotton yarn (double knitting/8 ply thickness)
- ♥ blue sparkle denim, 30 x 19cm (11¾ x 7½in) per mitten
- ♥ pink wool fabric 30 x 19cm (11¾ x 7½in) per mitten
- ♥ bright pompoms for hats
- ♥ silver-and-black striped bias binding 2.5cm (1in) wide – measure to the required length of your garland (you will need two equal sized lengths of binding for this project), plus ties at the ends
- ♥ grey embroidery thread
- ♥ toy stuffing
- ♥ sewing thread

Tools

- ♥ scissors (paper and fabric)
- ♥ sewing machine
- ♥ hand sewing needles
- ♥ pompom makers – small, medium and large
- ♥ card or craft paper
- ♥ tailor's chalk
- ♥ pins

1 Transfer the enlarged templates on page 64 onto card or craft paper and cut out. For the mittens, fold the blue sparkle denim or pink wool fabric in half, with right sides together. Draw around the enlarged template from page 64 with chalk, pin to hold and cut out. Machine stitch around the mitten, stitching 1cm (³/₈in) away from the raw edge and leaving the straight edge open to allow stuffing and turning through. Clip and trim the excess seam allowance and turn through. Stuff with toy stuffing. To close, turn 1cm (³/₈in) inwards along the opening. Make sure you insert one end of the knitted braid before closing by machine. Repeat for both mittens.

2 For the bobble hat, fold the beige jersey in half with, right sides together. Draw around the enlarged template from page 64 and pin to hold. Cut out and attach some fancy bias along the straight edges. Pin the pieces, right sides together, and machine stitch round the work, leaving the straight edge open. Trim the excess seam allowance and turn through. Stuff the hat with toy stuffing and slip stitch the opening closed. Sew a pompom to the top to finish.

3 For the scarf, trim the long edges of the thick checked wool with some fancy bias binding and press flat.

4 To make the fringed edges simply thread a needle with cotton yarn and sew through 1cm (³⁄₈in) from the edge looping the yarn over your finger as you go. Once you have reached the end, lay the loops flat and cut to the desired length, cutting straight across. Add a decorative stitch above the fringe line.

5 For the pompoms, follow the instructions at the front of this book (see page 17) and make as many as you like from white wool. Leave a decent amount of loose wool to attach them to the bunting.

6 Lastly, machine sew two lengths of bias binding together as close to the edges as possible. Press flat. Place all the elements in position and slip stitch. Suspend the hats with grey embroidery thread and simply tie the mittens in place.

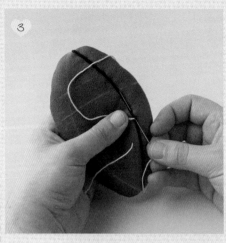

Sporty Garland

Materials

- ♥ templates for project on page 63
- ♥ polystyrene/styrofoam ball, 4cm (1½in) per shuttlecock
- ♥ 7 marabou feathers per shuttlecock
- ♥ red grosgrain ribbon, 30cm (12in) per shuttlecock
- ♥ cream cotton fabric, 11 x 11cm (4¼ x 4¼in) shuttlecock, 21 x 15cm (8¼ x 6in) per football and 13 x 13cm (5 x 5 in) per tennis ball
- ♥ bright green felt, 13 x 13cm (5 x 5in) per tennis ball
- ♥ brown wool, 21 x 15cm (8¼ x 6in) per football
- ♥ 1cm (⅜in) thick cream grosgrain ribbon, 10cm (4in) per ball
- ♥ bright blue cotton grosgrain ribbon 1.5cm (⅝in) wide
  – measure to the length required for your garland, plus ties at the ends
- ♥ cotton cream webbing tape 24cm (9½in) per football
- ♥ sewing thread
- ♥ white, black and cream embroidery thread

Tools

- ♥ scissors (paper and fabric)
- ♥ sewing machine
- ♥ hand sewing needles
- ♥ card or craft paper
- ♥ tailor's chalk
- ♥ pins
- ♥ pencil
- ♥ glue gun
- ♥ upholstery needle

1 Transfer the enlarged football and tennis ball templates on page 63 onto card or craft paper and cut out. Draw round the templates for both on cream cotton fabric with a pencil and cut out.

2 To make the football, lay the cotton piece you have cut out, pencil side up, on the brown wool and pin the fabric together. Prepare as many balls as you wish to make Set up your sewing machine and sew all round each ball 1cm ($^3/_8$in) from the edge, leaving no opening. Cut around the stitch lines, leaving a 5mm (¼in) seam allowance. Lightly clip the curves to avoid twisting when turning through. With the cotton side facing you, slash a straight line about 7cm (2¾in) long with fabric scissors. Turn the work through and use the blunt end of an upholstery needle to ease the shape of the ball out. To cover up the slashed opening, draw the fabric together with a large rough stitch. Cover the hole using the cream grosgrain ribbon. Slip stitch the ribbon in place for neatness. To make the tennis ball, repeat the same process layering the cream cotton peice that you cut for the tennis ball on to green felt.

3 Use the templates to chalk guidelines for the embroidery stitches on each football. Once chalked, stitch along the lines of the brown wool with black and yellow embroidery thread. Secure to finish. The decoration on the tennis ball is achieved in the same way using white embroidery thread.

4 Additionally, add some cotton webbing tape at either end of the football. Curve into position and slip stitch to secure. Finish at rear.

5 To make the shuttlecock, use the enlarged shuttlecock template from page 63 to mark and cut out a piece in cream cotton. Work a line of running stitch 5mm (¼in) away from the raw edge leaving the thread ends loose to gather. Place a 4cm (1½in) polystyrene ball in the centre and gather the cotton around the ball. Tie to secure.

6 With a glue gun, stick the marabou feathers around the ball, covering the raw edges of the cotton. To hide the feather tips, glue one end of the red grosgrain ribbon and wrap the length around the ball. When you come to the end, carefully glue the remaining tip down.

7 Lay out the blue cotton ribbon flat and position the shuttlecocks, tennis balls and footballs. Once you are happy with the spacing and placement, slip stitch in place.

Dream Land

Materials

- ♥ templates for projects on page 62
- ♥ cream cotton fabric, 18 x 22cm (7 x 8¾in) per moon, 16 x 20cm (6¼ x 7¾in) per bear, 28 x 14cm per star (11 x 5½in) per star
- ♥ yellow cotton, 18 x 22cm (7 x 8¾in) per moon
- ♥ blue sparkle denim, 28 x 14cm (11 x 5½in) per hat
- ♥ brown wool, 16 x 20cm (6¼ x 7¾in) per bear
- ♥ black and blue spotty cotton, 30 x 11cm (12 x 4¼in) per hat
- ♥ small yellow pompoms one per hat
- ♥ jumbo white ric rac ribbon, 4cm (1½in) wide
     – measure to the required length of your garland, plus ties at the ends
- ♥ 1cm (⅜in) thick cream grosgrain ribbon, 10cm (4in) per moon and bear
- ♥ sewing thread
- ♥ black embroidery thread

Tools

- ♥ scissors (paper and fabric)
- ♥ sewing machine
- ♥ glue gun
- ♥ hand sewing needles
- ♥ card or craft paper
- ♥ tailor's chalk
- ♥ pencil
- ♥ pins
- ♥ upholstery needle

1 With a pencil draw around the enlarged moon, bear and star templates on cream cotton fabric and cut out. Lay the cotton pencil side up onto the corresponding outer fabrics. Pin to hold and cut out.

2 Set up your sewing machine and sew all around each piece 1cm (⅜in) from the edge leaving no opening. Cut around the stitch lines, leaving a 5mm (¼in) seam allowance. Lightly clip the curves to avoid twisting when turning through. With the cotton side facing you, slash a straight line about 7cm (2¾in) long with fabric scissors (the exception to this is the stars, where you only need to slash around 4cm (1½in) in length - for the stars, slash one piece on its cream cotton side and one on the blue sparkle denim side).

3 Turn the work through and use the blunt end of an upholstery needle to ease out the shape. To cover up the slashed opening draw the fabric together with a large rough stitch. Cover the drawn hole using the grosgrain ribbon. Slip stitch the ribbon in place for neatness. When making the stars, there is no need to cover the openings with grosgain ribbon; match one triangle with the denim side slashed to one triangle with the cotton side slashed and glue them together (there should be two triangles per star).

4 To make the night hats, fold the spotty fabric in half, with right sides together. Using the enlarged nightcap template, draw around the marked lines with tailor's chalk and cut out. Pin the two layers together and machine stitch leaving the base of the cap open. Clip and turn the work through. Press flat. At the base, turn in 1cm (⅜in) and press. Add the nightcaps to the bears, moon and the odd star. Slip stitch in place around the base. To add character, fold the cap tip downwards, stitch to hold and glue a yellow pompom to the end.

5 Using the template, embroider the sleepy faces on the moons with black embroidery thread.

6 Arrange all the elements onto the white ric rac ribbon. Once you are happy with the placement, pin to hold. Flip the entire work over and slip stitch the pieces to the ribbon to secure.

Templates

Hot Air Balloon
Enlarge to 200%

Basket top

Basket base

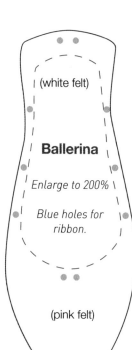

(white felt)

Ballerina

Enlarge to 200%

Blue holes for ribbon.

(pink felt)

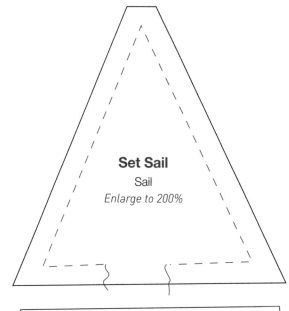

Set Sail
Sail
Enlarge to 200%

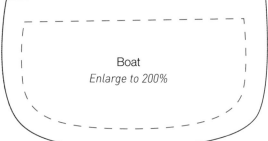

Boat
Enlarge to 200%

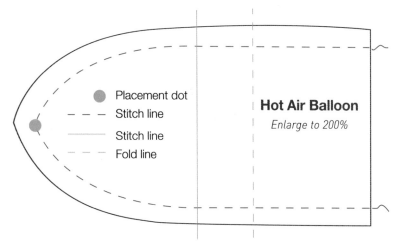

● Placement dot

- - - Stitch line

—— Stitch line

– – – Fold line

Hot Air Balloon
Enlarge to 200%

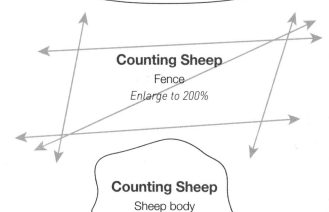

Counting Sheep
Fence
Enlarge to 200%

Counting Sheep
Sheep body
Enlarge to 200%

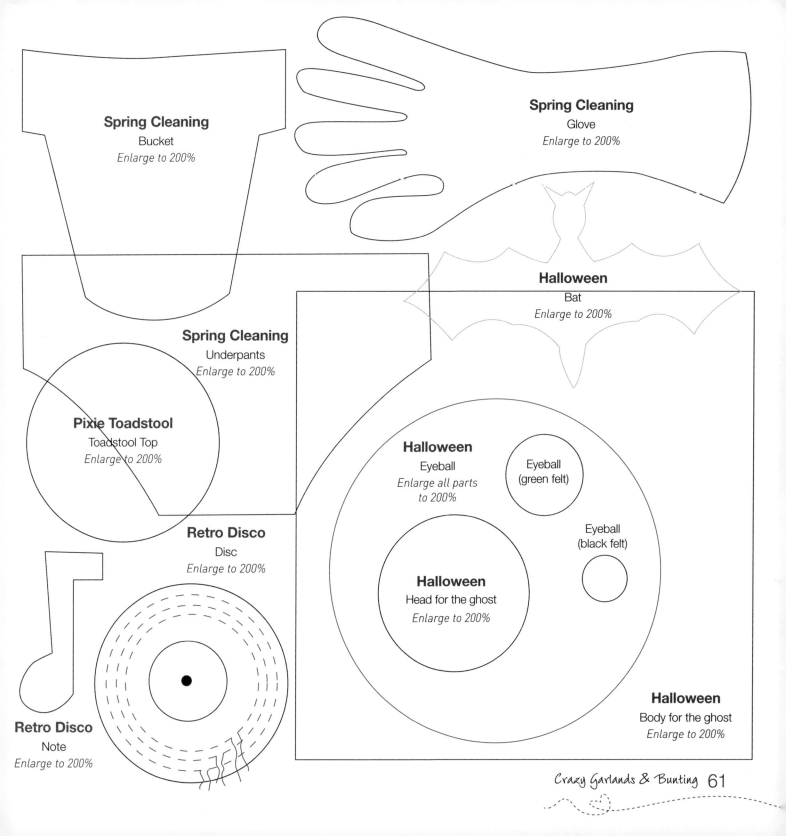

Spring Cleaning
Bucket
Enlarge to 200%

Spring Cleaning
Glove
Enlarge to 200%

Halloween
Bat
Enlarge to 200%

Spring Cleaning
Underpants
Enlarge to 200%

Pixie Toadstool
Toadstool Top
Enlarge to 200%

Halloween
Eyeball
*Enlarge all parts
to 200%*

Eyeball
(green felt)

Eyeball
(black felt)

Retro Disco
Disc
Enlarge to 200%

Halloween
Head for the ghost
Enlarge to 200%

Halloween
Body for the ghost
Enlarge to 200%

Retro Disco
Note
Enlarge to 200%

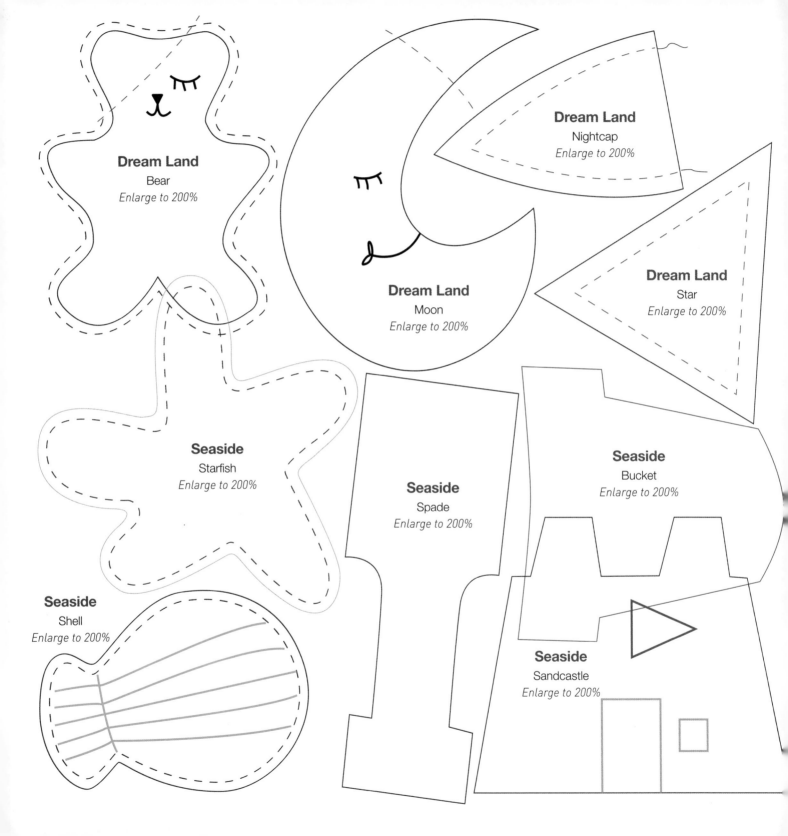

Dream Land
Bear
Enlarge to 200%

Dream Land
Nightcap
Enlarge to 200%

Dream Land
Moon
Enlarge to 200%

Dream Land
Star
Enlarge to 200%

Seaside
Starfish
Enlarge to 200%

Seaside
Spade
Enlarge to 200%

Seaside
Bucket
Enlarge to 200%

Seaside
Shell
Enlarge to 200%

Seaside
Sandcastle
Enlarge to 200%

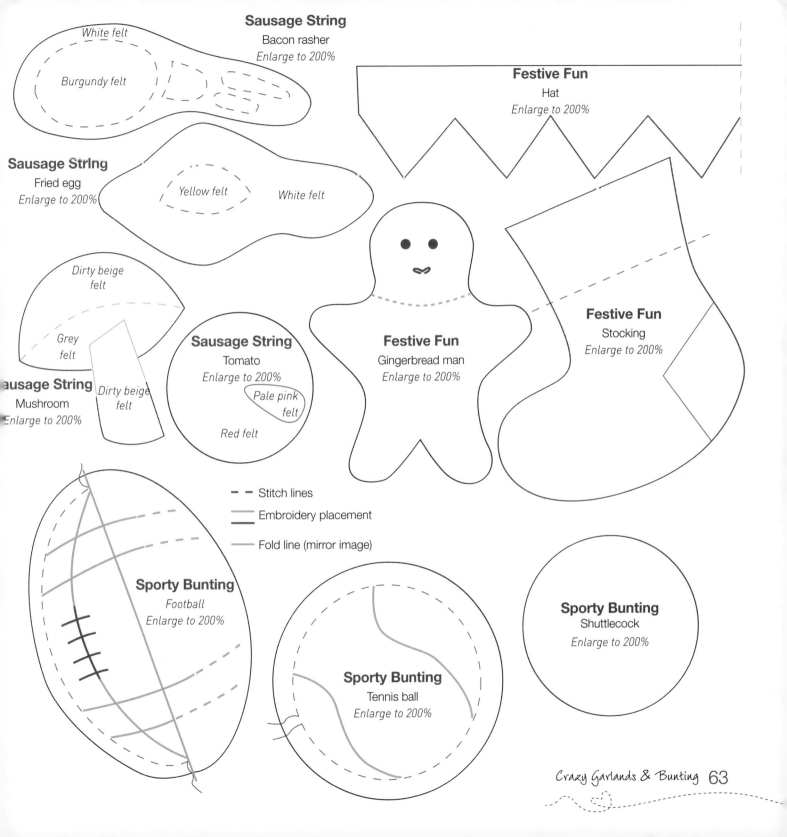

Sausage String

Bacon rasher
Enlarge to 200%

White felt

Burgundy felt

Festive Fun

Hat
Enlarge to 200%

Sausage String

Fried egg
Enlarge to 200%

Yellow felt

White felt

Festive Fun

Stocking
Enlarge to 200%

Dirty beige
felt

Grey
felt

Sausage String

Mushroom
Enlarge to 200%

Dirty beige
felt

Sausage String

Tomato
Enlarge to 200%

Pale pink
felt

Red felt

Festive Fun

Gingerbread man
Enlarge to 200%

– – – Stitch lines

⎯⎯ Embroidery placement

⎯⎯ Fold line (mirror image)

Sporty Bunting

Football
Enlarge to 200%

Sporty Bunting

Tennis ball
Enlarge to 200%

Sporty Bunting

Shuttlecock

Enlarge to 200%

Crazy Garlands & Bunting 63

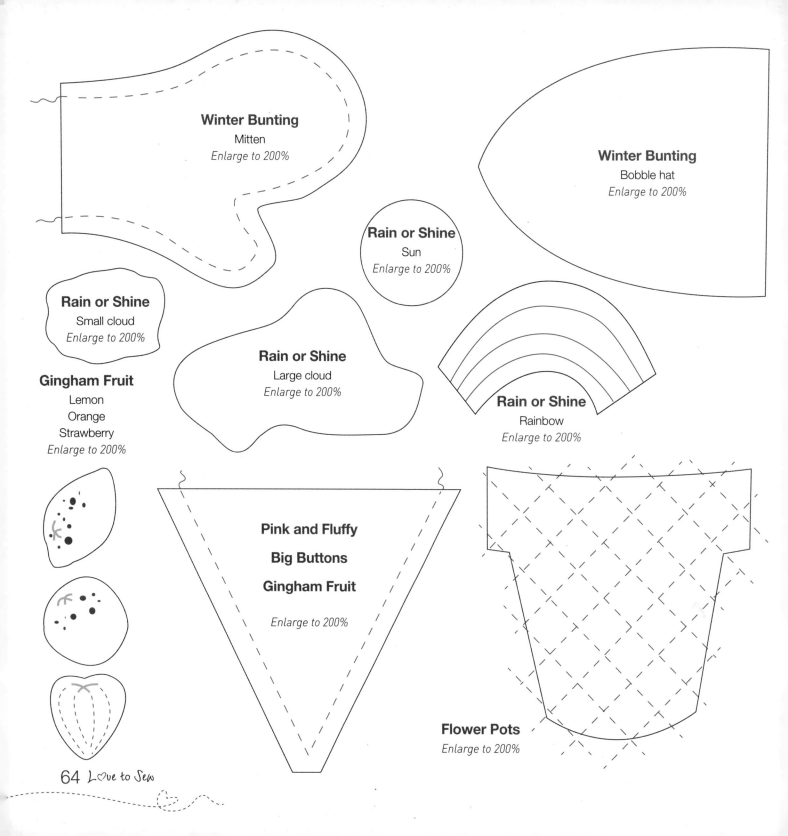

Winter Bunting
Mitten
Enlarge to 200%

Winter Bunting
Bobble hat
Enlarge to 200%

Rain or Shine
Sun
Enlarge to 200%

Rain or Shine
Small cloud
Enlarge to 200%

Rain or Shine
Large cloud
Enlarge to 200%

Rain or Shine
Rainbow
Enlarge to 200%

Gingham Fruit
Lemon
Orange
Strawberry
Enlarge to 200%

Pink and Fluffy

Big Buttons

Gingham Fruit

Enlarge to 200%

Flower Pots
Enlarge to 200%